50 Quick and Easy Freezer Meal Recipes for Home

By: Kelly Johnson

Table of Contents

- Chicken Parmesan Casserole
- Beef and Vegetable Stir-Fry
- Spinach and Feta Stuffed Chicken Breast
- Vegetarian Chili
- Teriyaki Salmon
- Lentil Soup
- Cheesy Broccoli and Rice Casserole
- BBQ Pulled Pork
- Chicken Alfredo Pasta Bake
- Black Bean and Corn Quesadillas
- Sweet Potato and Chickpea Curry
- Turkey and Veggie Meatballs
- Vegetable Lasagna
- Sausage and Peppers
- Creamy Tomato Basil Soup
- Honey Garlic Chicken
- Eggplant Parmesan
- Shrimp and Broccoli Alfredo
- Mexican Quinoa Casserole
- Spaghetti Bolognese
- Chicken and Rice Burritos
- Vegetable and Chickpea Stew
- Taco Soup
- Mushroom and Spinach Stuffed Shells
- Orange Ginger Glazed Chicken
- Cauliflower Fried Rice
- Beef and Black Bean Enchiladas
- Creamy Pesto Chicken Pasta
- Butternut Squash Soup
- Salmon and Asparagus Foil Packets
- Vegetarian Enchilada Casserole
- Sesame Ginger Beef Stir-Fry
- Chicken and Broccoli Bake
- Mediterranean Quinoa Salad
- Turkey and Vegetable Chili

- Caprese Stuffed Chicken
- Honey Mustard Glazed Pork Chops
- Chicken and Rice Casserole
- Vegetable and Lentil Curry
- Cilantro Lime Shrimp
- Greek Chicken Souvlaki
- Macaroni and Cheese with Broccoli
- Asian Peanut Noodles with Tofu
- Baked Ziti
- Moroccan Chickpea Stew
- Buffalo Chicken Wraps
- Vegetarian Spinach and Mushroom Enchiladas
- Cabbage Roll Casserole
- Lemon Herb Grilled Chicken
- Sweet and Sour Meatballs

Chicken Parmesan Casserole

Ingredients:

- 2 lbs boneless, skinless chicken breasts, cooked and shredded
- 2 cups marinara sauce
- 1 cup mozzarella cheese, shredded
- 1 cup Parmesan cheese, grated
- 1 cup breadcrumbs
- 1/2 cup fresh basil, chopped
- 1/4 cup olive oil
- 3 cloves garlic, minced
- 1 teaspoon dried oregano
- Salt and pepper to taste
- 1/4 cup fresh parsley, chopped (for garnish)

Instructions:

Preheat your oven to 375°F (190°C).
In a large mixing bowl, combine the shredded chicken, marinara sauce, half of the mozzarella, half of the Parmesan, and chopped basil. Mix until well combined.
In a separate bowl, mix the breadcrumbs, remaining mozzarella, remaining Parmesan, minced garlic, dried oregano, salt, and pepper.
Grease a baking dish with olive oil. Place half of the breadcrumb mixture on the bottom of the dish, creating an even layer.
Spread the chicken mixture evenly over the breadcrumb layer.
Top the chicken mixture with the remaining breadcrumb mixture.
Drizzle olive oil over the top of the casserole.
Bake in the preheated oven for 25-30 minutes or until the top is golden brown and the casserole is bubbly.
Remove from the oven and let it cool for a few minutes.
Garnish with fresh parsley before serving.
Serve the Chicken Parmesan Casserole over cooked pasta, rice, or with a side of crusty bread.

Enjoy this easy and delicious freezer-friendly Chicken Parmesan Casserole!

Beef and Vegetable Stir-Fry

Ingredients:

- 1 lb flank steak, thinly sliced
- 2 tablespoons soy sauce
- 1 tablespoon oyster sauce
- 1 tablespoon hoisin sauce
- 2 teaspoons cornstarch
- 1 tablespoon vegetable oil
- 3 cups broccoli florets
- 1 bell pepper, thinly sliced
- 1 carrot, julienned
- 1 cup snap peas, trimmed
- 3 cloves garlic, minced
- 1 tablespoon fresh ginger, grated
- 2 green onions, sliced (for garnish)
- Sesame seeds (optional, for garnish)
- Cooked rice or noodles (for serving)

Instructions:

In a bowl, mix together soy sauce, oyster sauce, hoisin sauce, and cornstarch.
Add sliced flank steak to the mixture, ensuring the beef is well coated. Allow it to marinate for at least 15-20 minutes.
Heat vegetable oil in a wok or large skillet over medium-high heat.
Add marinated beef to the hot wok and stir-fry for 2-3 minutes or until browned.
Remove the beef from the wok and set it aside.
In the same wok, add a bit more oil if needed. Stir in garlic and ginger, cooking for about 1 minute until fragrant.
Add broccoli, bell pepper, carrot, and snap peas to the wok. Stir-fry the vegetables for 4-5 minutes or until they are crisp-tender.
Return the cooked beef to the wok with the vegetables. Stir everything together and cook for an additional 2-3 minutes.
Taste and adjust seasoning if necessary.
Serve the beef and vegetable stir-fry over cooked rice or noodles.
Garnish with sliced green onions and sesame seeds if desired.
Enjoy your quick and flavorful beef and vegetable stir-fry!

This dish freezes well after cooking. Allow it to cool completely before transferring to freezer-friendly containers. To reheat, simply thaw and stir-fry in a hot wok or skillet until warmed through.

Spinach and Feta Stuffed Chicken Breast

Ingredients:

- 4 boneless, skinless chicken breasts
- 2 cups fresh spinach, chopped
- 1/2 cup feta cheese, crumbled
- 1/4 cup sun-dried tomatoes, chopped (optional)
- 2 cloves garlic, minced
- 1 tablespoon olive oil
- 1 teaspoon dried oregano
- Salt and pepper to taste
- Toothpicks or kitchen twine
- Lemon wedges (for serving)

Instructions:

Preheat the oven to 375°F (190°C).
In a skillet, heat olive oil over medium heat. Add minced garlic and sauté for 1-2 minutes until fragrant.
Add chopped spinach to the skillet and cook until wilted, about 2-3 minutes. Remove from heat.
In a bowl, combine the wilted spinach, crumbled feta, and sun-dried tomatoes (if using). Mix well.
Lay the chicken breasts on a cutting board and make a horizontal slit along the side of each breast to create a pocket.
Stuff each chicken breast with the spinach and feta mixture. Use toothpicks or kitchen twine to secure the openings and keep the stuffing in place.
Season the outside of each stuffed chicken breast with dried oregano, salt, and pepper.
Heat a bit of olive oil in an oven-safe skillet over medium-high heat.
Sear the stuffed chicken breasts on each side for 2-3 minutes until golden brown.
Transfer the skillet to the preheated oven and bake for 20-25 minutes or until the chicken is cooked through.
Remove from the oven and let it rest for a few minutes before serving.
Serve the spinach and feta stuffed chicken breasts with lemon wedges on the side.

Enjoy this delicious and elegant freezer-friendly dish! To freeze, allow the stuffed chicken breasts to cool completely before wrapping tightly in plastic wrap or aluminum foil. Thaw in the refrigerator before reheating in the oven.

Vegetarian Chili

Ingredients:

- 2 tablespoons olive oil
- 1 large onion, diced
- 3 cloves garlic, minced
- 1 bell pepper, diced (any color)
- 1 zucchini, diced
- 1 carrot, diced
- 1 can (15 oz) black beans, drained and rinsed
- 1 can (15 oz) kidney beans, drained and rinsed
- 1 can (15 oz) pinto beans, drained and rinsed
- 1 can (28 oz) crushed tomatoes
- 1 can (15 oz) diced tomatoes
- 2 cups vegetable broth
- 2 tablespoons tomato paste
- 2 teaspoons ground cumin
- 1 tablespoon chili powder
- 1 teaspoon paprika
- 1 teaspoon oregano
- Salt and pepper to taste
- 1 cup frozen corn kernels
- 1 tablespoon lime juice
- Fresh cilantro, chopped (for garnish)
- Shredded cheddar cheese (optional, for topping)
- Sour cream or Greek yogurt (optional, for topping)
- Sliced green onions (optional, for topping)

Instructions:

In a large pot, heat olive oil over medium heat. Add diced onion, garlic, bell pepper, zucchini, and carrot. Sauté until the vegetables are softened, about 5-7 minutes.

Add crushed tomatoes, diced tomatoes, black beans, kidney beans, pinto beans, vegetable broth, and tomato paste to the pot. Stir to combine.

Season the chili with cumin, chili powder, paprika, oregano, salt, and pepper. Mix well.

Bring the mixture to a simmer, then reduce the heat to low. Cover and let it simmer for at least 20-30 minutes to allow the flavors to meld together.

Add frozen corn kernels and lime juice to the chili. Stir and let it simmer for an additional 10 minutes.

Taste and adjust the seasoning as needed.

Serve the vegetarian chili hot, garnished with chopped cilantro. If desired, top with shredded cheddar cheese, sour cream or Greek yogurt, and sliced green onions.

Allow any leftovers to cool before transferring to freezer-safe containers.

This hearty and flavorful vegetarian chili is perfect for freezing. When reheating, you may need to add a bit of extra vegetable broth to achieve your preferred consistency.

Enjoy!

Teriyaki Salmon

Ingredients:

- 4 salmon fillets
- 1/2 cup soy sauce
- 1/4 cup mirin (Japanese sweet rice wine)
- 2 tablespoons sake (or white wine)
- 2 tablespoons brown sugar
- 1 tablespoon honey
- 1 tablespoon sesame oil
- 3 cloves garlic, minced
- 1 tablespoon fresh ginger, grated
- 2 green onions, sliced (for garnish)
- Sesame seeds (for garnish)
- Cooked white or brown rice (for serving)
- Steamed broccoli or vegetables (optional, for serving)

Instructions:

In a bowl, whisk together soy sauce, mirin, sake, brown sugar, honey, sesame oil, minced garlic, and grated ginger to create the teriyaki sauce.

Place the salmon fillets in a shallow dish or a resealable plastic bag. Pour half of the teriyaki sauce over the salmon, ensuring each fillet is coated. Reserve the other half for later.

Marinate the salmon for at least 30 minutes, or for more flavor, marinate in the refrigerator for up to 4 hours.

Preheat your oven to 400°F (200°C).

Place the marinated salmon fillets on a baking sheet lined with parchment paper. Bake for 15-20 minutes or until the salmon is cooked through and flakes easily with a fork.

While the salmon is baking, transfer the reserved teriyaki sauce to a small saucepan. Simmer over medium heat until it thickens, stirring occasionally.

Once the salmon is done, brush the thickened teriyaki sauce over the fillets.

Serve the teriyaki salmon over cooked rice, garnished with sliced green onions and sesame seeds.

Optional: Serve with steamed broccoli or your favorite vegetables on the side. Enjoy this delicious and easy teriyaki salmon!

To freeze, let the cooked teriyaki salmon cool completely before placing it in airtight containers. When reheating, consider drizzling with a bit of extra teriyaki sauce for added flavor.

Lentil Soup

Ingredients:

- 2 cups dried green or brown lentils, rinsed and drained
- 1 onion, finely chopped
- 2 carrots, peeled and diced
- 2 celery stalks, diced
- 3 cloves garlic, minced
- 1 can (14 oz) diced tomatoes
- 6 cups vegetable broth
- 1 teaspoon ground cumin
- 1 teaspoon ground coriander
- 1 teaspoon smoked paprika
- 1/2 teaspoon ground turmeric
- 1 bay leaf
- Salt and pepper to taste
- 2 tablespoons olive oil
- Juice of 1 lemon
- Fresh parsley, chopped (for garnish)

Instructions:

In a large pot, heat olive oil over medium heat. Add chopped onions, carrots, and celery. Sauté until the vegetables are softened, about 5 minutes.

Add minced garlic to the pot and sauté for an additional 1-2 minutes until fragrant.

Pour in the vegetable broth and add the lentils, diced tomatoes, ground cumin, ground coriander, smoked paprika, ground turmeric, bay leaf, salt, and pepper. Stir to combine.

Bring the soup to a boil, then reduce the heat to low. Cover and let it simmer for about 25-30 minutes or until the lentils are tender.

Remove the bay leaf and discard it.

Stir in the lemon juice to brighten the flavors.

Taste and adjust the seasoning if needed.

Optional: Use an immersion blender to partially blend the soup for a thicker consistency.

Serve the lentil soup hot, garnished with fresh parsley.

Allow any leftover soup to cool completely before transferring to freezer-safe containers.

This lentil soup is not only delicious but also freezes well. Reheat on the stovetop or in the microwave for a quick and comforting meal. Enjoy!

Cheesy Broccoli and Rice Casserole

Ingredients:

- 2 cups broccoli florets, blanched
- 2 cups cooked white rice
- 2 cups shredded cheddar cheese
- 1 cup sour cream
- 1/2 cup mayonnaise
- 1 small onion, finely chopped
- 2 cloves garlic, minced
- 1 teaspoon Dijon mustard
- Salt and pepper to taste
- 1 cup breadcrumbs
- 2 tablespoons unsalted butter, melted
- Fresh parsley, chopped (for garnish)

Instructions:

Preheat your oven to 350°F (175°C). Grease a baking dish with butter or cooking spray.
In a large mixing bowl, combine blanched broccoli, cooked rice, shredded cheddar cheese, chopped onion, and minced garlic.
In a separate bowl, mix together sour cream, mayonnaise, Dijon mustard, salt, and pepper.
Pour the sour cream mixture over the broccoli and rice mixture. Mix until well combined.
Transfer the mixture to the prepared baking dish, spreading it out evenly.
In a small bowl, combine breadcrumbs with melted butter.
Sprinkle the breadcrumb mixture evenly over the casserole.
Bake in the preheated oven for 25-30 minutes or until the casserole is hot and bubbly, and the breadcrumbs are golden brown.
Remove from the oven and let it rest for a few minutes.
Garnish with chopped fresh parsley before serving.
Serve the cheesy broccoli and rice casserole as a delicious side dish or a comforting main course.
Allow any leftovers to cool before transferring to freezer-safe containers.

This cheesy broccoli and rice casserole is a crowd-pleaser and can be easily reheated from the freezer for a quick meal. Enjoy!

BBQ Pulled Pork

Ingredients:

- 3-4 lbs pork shoulder or pork butt
- 1 large onion, sliced
- 4 cloves garlic, minced
- 1 cup barbecue sauce (plus extra for serving)
- 1/2 cup apple cider vinegar
- 1/2 cup chicken or vegetable broth
- 2 tablespoons brown sugar
- 1 tablespoon Dijon mustard
- 1 tablespoon Worcestershire sauce
- 1 teaspoon smoked paprika
- 1 teaspoon chili powder
- Salt and pepper to taste
- Hamburger buns or rolls (for serving)
- Coleslaw (optional, for topping)

Instructions:

Trim excess fat from the pork shoulder, and season it with salt and pepper.
In a mixing bowl, whisk together barbecue sauce, apple cider vinegar, broth, brown sugar, Dijon mustard, Worcestershire sauce, smoked paprika, and chili powder to create the BBQ sauce.
Place sliced onions and minced garlic in the bottom of a slow cooker.
Put the seasoned pork shoulder on top of the onions and garlic.
Pour the BBQ sauce over the pork, ensuring it's well-coated.
Cook on low for 8-10 hours or on high for 4-6 hours until the pork is tender and easily shreds.
Once cooked, use two forks to shred the pork directly in the slow cooker, mixing it with the sauce.
Taste and adjust the seasoning if necessary.
Serve the BBQ pulled pork on hamburger buns or rolls, topped with extra barbecue sauce and coleslaw if desired.
Allow any leftovers to cool before transferring to freezer-safe containers.

This BBQ pulled pork is not only great for serving a crowd but also freezes well for later enjoyment. Reheat it on the stovetop or in the microwave, and you'll have a delicious meal in no time. Enjoy!

Chicken Alfredo Pasta Bake

Ingredients:

- 1 lb penne pasta, cooked according to package instructions
- 2 cups cooked and shredded chicken breast
- 2 cups broccoli florets, blanched
- 2 cups shredded mozzarella cheese
- 1 cup grated Parmesan cheese
- 2 cups Alfredo sauce (store-bought or homemade)
- 1/2 cup chicken broth
- 3 cloves garlic, minced
- 1 teaspoon dried oregano
- Salt and pepper to taste
- Fresh parsley, chopped (for garnish)

Instructions:

Preheat your oven to 375°F (190°C). Grease a baking dish with butter or cooking spray.

In a large mixing bowl, combine the cooked penne pasta, shredded chicken, blanched broccoli, mozzarella cheese, and Parmesan cheese.

In a saucepan over medium heat, combine Alfredo sauce, chicken broth, minced garlic, dried oregano, salt, and pepper. Heat until warmed through and well combined.

Pour the Alfredo sauce mixture over the pasta and chicken mixture. Toss everything together until evenly coated.

Transfer the pasta mixture to the prepared baking dish, spreading it out evenly.

Bake in the preheated oven for 25-30 minutes or until the top is golden brown and the pasta is bubbly.

Remove from the oven and let it rest for a few minutes.

Garnish with chopped fresh parsley before serving.

Serve the Chicken Alfredo Pasta Bake as a comforting and hearty meal.

Allow any leftovers to cool before transferring to freezer-safe containers.

This Chicken Alfredo Pasta Bake is a delightful freezer-friendly dish that can be reheated in the oven or microwave. Enjoy the creamy and cheesy goodness!

Black Bean and Corn Quesadillas

Ingredients:

- 1 can (15 oz) black beans, drained and rinsed
- 1 cup corn kernels (fresh, frozen, or canned)
- 1 cup diced bell peppers (any color)
- 1 cup shredded cheddar cheese
- 1 cup shredded Monterey Jack cheese
- 1/2 cup diced red onion
- 1/4 cup chopped fresh cilantro
- 1 teaspoon ground cumin
- 1 teaspoon chili powder
- Salt and pepper to taste
- 8 medium-sized flour tortillas
- Olive oil or cooking spray
- Salsa, sour cream, or guacamole (for serving)

Instructions:

In a bowl, combine black beans, corn, diced bell peppers, shredded cheddar cheese, shredded Monterey Jack cheese, diced red onion, chopped cilantro, ground cumin, chili powder, salt, and pepper. Mix well.
Heat a large skillet over medium heat.
Place a tortilla in the skillet and spoon a portion of the black bean and corn mixture onto one half of the tortilla.
Fold the other half of the tortilla over the filling, creating a half-moon shape.
Press down gently with a spatula and cook for 2-3 minutes on each side or until the tortilla is golden brown and the cheese is melted.
Repeat the process for the remaining tortillas and filling.
If needed, add a little olive oil or use cooking spray between batches to prevent sticking.
Once all quesadillas are cooked, allow them to cool for a few minutes before slicing into wedges.
Serve the Black Bean and Corn Quesadillas with salsa, sour cream, or guacamole on the side.
Allow any leftovers to cool before transferring to freezer-safe containers, separating quesadillas with parchment paper for easy reheating.

Enjoy these flavorful and satisfying quesadillas, perfect for a quick meal or snack!

Sweet Potato and Chickpea Curry

Ingredients:

- 2 medium-sized sweet potatoes, peeled and diced
- 1 can (15 oz) chickpeas, drained and rinsed
- 1 large onion, finely chopped
- 3 cloves garlic, minced
- 1 tablespoon fresh ginger, grated
- 1 can (14 oz) diced tomatoes
- 1 can (14 oz) coconut milk
- 2 tablespoons curry powder
- 1 teaspoon ground cumin
- 1 teaspoon ground coriander
- 1/2 teaspoon turmeric
- 1/2 teaspoon cayenne pepper (adjust to taste)
- Salt and pepper to taste
- 2 tablespoons olive oil
- Fresh cilantro, chopped (for garnish)
- Cooked rice or naan bread (for serving)

Instructions:

In a large pot or deep skillet, heat olive oil over medium heat. Add chopped onions and sauté until they become translucent.
Add minced garlic and grated ginger to the pot. Sauté for an additional 1-2 minutes until fragrant.
Stir in curry powder, ground cumin, ground coriander, turmeric, cayenne pepper, salt, and pepper. Mix well to coat the onions, garlic, and ginger with the spices.
Add diced sweet potatoes, chickpeas, diced tomatoes (with their juice), and coconut milk to the pot. Stir to combine.
Bring the mixture to a simmer, then reduce the heat to low. Cover and let it simmer for about 20-25 minutes or until the sweet potatoes are tender.
Taste and adjust the seasoning if necessary.
Serve the Sweet Potato and Chickpea Curry over cooked rice or with naan bread. Garnish with chopped fresh cilantro.
Allow any leftovers to cool before transferring to freezer-safe containers.

This Sweet Potato and Chickpea Curry is a nutritious and satisfying dish that freezes well. Reheat it on the stovetop or in the microwave for a quick and flavorful meal. Enjoy!

Turkey and Veggie Meatballs

Ingredients:

For the Meatballs:

- 1 lb ground turkey
- 1 cup zucchini, grated and squeezed to remove excess moisture
- 1 cup carrots, grated
- 1/2 cup onion, finely chopped
- 2 cloves garlic, minced
- 1/2 cup breadcrumbs
- 1/4 cup Parmesan cheese, grated
- 1 large egg
- 1 teaspoon dried oregano
- 1 teaspoon dried basil
- Salt and pepper to taste
- Olive oil (for greasing)

For the Sauce:

- 1 can (15 oz) crushed tomatoes
- 1 clove garlic, minced
- 1 teaspoon dried Italian herbs (basil, oregano, thyme)
- Salt and pepper to taste

Instructions:

Preheat the oven to 400°F (200°C). Grease a baking sheet with olive oil.
In a large bowl, combine ground turkey, grated zucchini, grated carrots, chopped onion, minced garlic, breadcrumbs, Parmesan cheese, egg, dried oregano, dried basil, salt, and pepper. Mix until well combined.
Shape the mixture into meatballs, about 1 to 1.5 inches in diameter, and place them on the prepared baking sheet.
Bake the meatballs in the preheated oven for 20-25 minutes or until they are cooked through and browned on the outside.
While the meatballs are baking, prepare the sauce. In a saucepan, combine crushed tomatoes, minced garlic, dried Italian herbs, salt, and pepper. Simmer over low heat for about 10-15 minutes.

Once the meatballs are done, add them to the sauce, allowing them to simmer together for an additional 5 minutes.
Serve the Turkey and Veggie Meatballs over cooked pasta or as a sub sandwich filling.
Allow any leftovers to cool before transferring to freezer-safe containers.

These turkey and veggie meatballs are a healthier alternative and can be easily frozen for future meals. Reheat them on the stovetop or in the microwave, and enjoy!

Vegetable Lasagna

Ingredients:

For the Filling:

- 9 lasagna noodles, cooked according to package instructions
- 1 large eggplant, thinly sliced
- 2 zucchini, thinly sliced
- 1 yellow bell pepper, thinly sliced
- 1 red bell pepper, thinly sliced
- 1 cup mushrooms, sliced
- 1 large onion, finely chopped
- 3 cloves garlic, minced
- 2 cups spinach, chopped
- 1 can (28 oz) crushed tomatoes
- 1 can (14 oz) diced tomatoes
- 1 teaspoon dried oregano
- 1 teaspoon dried basil
- Salt and pepper to taste
- 2 tablespoons olive oil

For the Cheese Mixture:

- 2 cups ricotta cheese
- 1 cup mozzarella cheese, shredded
- 1/2 cup Parmesan cheese, grated
- 1 large egg
- Salt and pepper to taste

For Assembly:

- 2 cups mozzarella cheese, shredded (for topping)
- Fresh basil or parsley, chopped (for garnish)

Instructions:

Preheat the oven to 375°F (190°C). Grease a 9x13-inch baking dish.

In a large skillet, heat olive oil over medium heat. Add chopped onion and minced garlic, sautéing until translucent.

Add sliced eggplant, zucchini, bell peppers, mushrooms, and chopped spinach to the skillet. Cook until the vegetables are tender.

Stir in crushed tomatoes, diced tomatoes, dried oregano, dried basil, salt, and pepper. Simmer the vegetable mixture for about 15-20 minutes, allowing the flavors to meld.

In a separate bowl, mix together ricotta cheese, mozzarella cheese, Parmesan cheese, egg, salt, and pepper to create the cheese mixture.

To assemble the lasagna, spread a thin layer of the vegetable sauce in the bottom of the prepared baking dish. Place three lasagna noodles on top.

Spread half of the cheese mixture over the noodles, followed by half of the vegetable mixture.

Repeat the layers: noodles, remaining cheese mixture, and remaining vegetable mixture.

Top with a final layer of lasagna noodles and sprinkle the top with shredded mozzarella cheese.

Cover the baking dish with aluminum foil and bake in the preheated oven for 25-30 minutes.

Remove the foil and bake for an additional 10-15 minutes or until the top is golden brown and the lasagna is bubbly.

Let the vegetable lasagna cool for a few minutes before slicing.

Garnish with fresh basil or parsley before serving.

Allow any leftovers to cool before transferring to freezer-safe containers.

This vegetable lasagna is a hearty and flavorful dish that freezes well for convenient future meals. Reheat in the oven or microwave, and enjoy!

Sausage and Peppers

Ingredients:

- 1 lb Italian sausage links (sweet or hot), sliced
- 2 bell peppers (any color), sliced
- 1 large onion, sliced
- 3 cloves garlic, minced
- 1 can (14 oz) crushed tomatoes
- 1 teaspoon dried oregano
- 1 teaspoon dried basil
- 1/2 teaspoon red pepper flakes (optional, for heat)
- Salt and black pepper to taste
- 2 tablespoons olive oil
- Fresh basil or parsley, chopped (for garnish)
- Crusty Italian bread or rolls (for serving)

Instructions:

Heat olive oil in a large skillet or pan over medium heat.
Add sliced sausage links to the skillet and cook until browned on all sides.
Remove the sausages from the skillet and set aside.
In the same skillet, add sliced bell peppers and onions. Sauté until they are softened and slightly caramelized.
Add minced garlic to the peppers and onions, sautéing for an additional 1-2 minutes until fragrant.
Pour in crushed tomatoes and add dried oregano, dried basil, red pepper flakes (if using), salt, and black pepper. Stir to combine.
Add the cooked sausages back to the skillet, nestling them into the pepper and onion mixture.
Simmer the sausage and peppers in the tomato sauce for 15-20 minutes, allowing the flavors to meld together.
Taste and adjust the seasoning if necessary.
Garnish with chopped fresh basil or parsley before serving.
Serve the sausage and peppers hot over crusty Italian bread or rolls.
Allow any leftovers to cool before transferring to freezer-safe containers.

This classic sausage and peppers dish is not only delicious but also freezes well for future meals. Reheat on the stovetop or in the microwave, and enjoy with your favorite bread!

Creamy Tomato Basil Soup

Ingredients:

- 2 tablespoons olive oil
- 1 onion, chopped
- 3 cloves garlic, minced
- 2 cans (28 oz each) crushed tomatoes
- 1 can (14 oz) diced tomatoes
- 4 cups vegetable or chicken broth
- 1 cup heavy cream
- 1/4 cup fresh basil, chopped
- 1 teaspoon dried oregano
- 1 teaspoon dried thyme
- Salt and pepper to taste
- 1/4 cup unsalted butter
- 1/4 cup all-purpose flour
- 1/2 cup grated Parmesan cheese
- Croutons or fresh basil (for garnish)

Instructions:

In a large pot, heat olive oil over medium heat. Add chopped onions and sauté until they become translucent.

Add minced garlic to the pot and sauté for an additional 1-2 minutes until fragrant.

Pour in crushed tomatoes, diced tomatoes, and vegetable or chicken broth. Stir well.

Add dried oregano, dried thyme, salt, and pepper to the pot. Bring the mixture to a simmer, then reduce the heat to low. Cover and let it simmer for about 20-25 minutes.

In a separate saucepan, melt unsalted butter over medium heat. Stir in all-purpose flour to create a roux. Cook for 2-3 minutes, stirring constantly.

Gradually whisk in heavy cream until the mixture is smooth and thickened.

Add the roux mixture to the soup, stirring well to combine. Simmer for an additional 10 minutes.

Stir in chopped fresh basil and grated Parmesan cheese. Taste and adjust the seasoning if necessary.

Using an immersion blender or transferring in batches to a blender, blend the soup until smooth.
Garnish with croutons or fresh basil before serving.
Allow any leftover soup to cool before transferring to freezer-safe containers.

This creamy tomato basil soup is a comforting classic that freezes well. Reheat it on the stovetop or in the microwave, and enjoy with your favorite crusty bread.

Honey Garlic Chicken

Ingredients:

- 4 boneless, skinless chicken breasts
- Salt and pepper to taste
- 1/2 cup honey
- 1/4 cup soy sauce
- 3 tablespoons garlic, minced
- 1 tablespoon ginger, grated
- 2 tablespoons olive oil
- Sesame seeds (for garnish)
- Green onions, chopped (for garnish)
- Cooked rice (for serving)

Instructions:

Season the chicken breasts with salt and pepper.
In a small bowl, whisk together honey, soy sauce, minced garlic, and grated ginger to create the marinade.
Place the chicken breasts in a resealable plastic bag or shallow dish. Pour half of the marinade over the chicken, reserving the rest for later. Seal the bag or cover the dish and let it marinate in the refrigerator for at least 30 minutes.
In a large skillet, heat olive oil over medium-high heat.
Remove the chicken from the marinade and cook in the skillet for about 6-7 minutes per side or until the internal temperature reaches 165°F (74°C) and the chicken is golden brown.
Pour the reserved marinade into the skillet and let it simmer for an additional 2-3 minutes, allowing it to thicken slightly.
Coat the chicken in the sauce, turning it to ensure it's well coated.
Garnish with sesame seeds and chopped green onions.
Serve the Honey Garlic Chicken over cooked rice.
Allow any leftovers to cool before transferring to freezer-safe containers.

This sweet and savory Honey Garlic Chicken is a quick and delicious meal that freezes well. Reheat in the oven or microwave for a tasty and convenient dish. Enjoy!

Eggplant Parmesan

Ingredients:

For the Eggplant:

- 2 large eggplants, sliced into 1/2-inch rounds
- Salt
- 2 cups all-purpose flour
- 4 large eggs, beaten
- 2 cups breadcrumbs
- 1 cup grated Parmesan cheese
- Olive oil (for frying)

For the Assembly:

- 3 cups marinara sauce (store-bought or homemade)
- 2 cups shredded mozzarella cheese
- 1/2 cup grated Parmesan cheese
- Fresh basil or parsley, chopped (for garnish)
- Cooked spaghetti or your favorite pasta (for serving)

Instructions:

Prepare the Eggplant:
- Sprinkle salt over the eggplant slices and let them sit for about 30 minutes. This helps remove excess moisture and bitterness. After 30 minutes, pat the eggplant slices dry with paper towels.
- Set up a breading station with three shallow dishes: one with flour, one with beaten eggs, and one with a mixture of breadcrumbs and grated Parmesan cheese.
- Dredge each eggplant slice in the flour, dip into the beaten eggs, and coat with the breadcrumb-Parmesan mixture, pressing gently to adhere.
- Heat olive oil in a large skillet over medium-high heat. Fry the breaded eggplant slices in batches until golden brown on both sides. Place them on a paper towel-lined plate to drain excess oil.

Assemble the Eggplant Parmesan:

- Preheat the oven to 375°F (190°C).
- Spread a thin layer of marinara sauce in the bottom of a baking dish.
- Arrange a layer of fried eggplant slices on top of the sauce.
- Spoon more marinara sauce over the eggplant and sprinkle with shredded mozzarella and grated Parmesan cheese.
- Repeat the layers until all the eggplant is used, finishing with a layer of sauce and cheese on top.

Bake:
- Cover the baking dish with aluminum foil and bake in the preheated oven for 25-30 minutes.
- Remove the foil and bake for an additional 10-15 minutes or until the cheese is melted and bubbly, and the top is golden brown.

Serve:
- Let the Eggplant Parmesan rest for a few minutes before serving.
- Garnish with chopped fresh basil or parsley.

Optional:
- Serve the Eggplant Parmesan over cooked spaghetti or your favorite pasta.

Freezing:
- Allow any leftovers to cool before transferring to freezer-safe containers.

This Eggplant Parmesan is a satisfying and flavorful dish that freezes well. Reheat it in the oven for a delicious and convenient meal. Enjoy!

Shrimp and Broccoli Alfredo

Ingredients:

- 1 lb shrimp, peeled and deveined
- 1 lb broccoli florets
- 1 lb fettuccine pasta
- 3 tablespoons unsalted butter
- 3 cloves garlic, minced
- 1 cup heavy cream
- 1 cup grated Parmesan cheese
- Salt and pepper to taste
- Red pepper flakes (optional, for heat)
- Fresh parsley, chopped (for garnish)
- Lemon wedges (for serving)

Instructions:

Cook the fettuccine pasta according to package instructions. Drain and set aside.
In a large pot of boiling salted water, blanch the broccoli florets for 2-3 minutes until slightly tender. Drain and set aside.
In a large skillet, melt the butter over medium heat. Add minced garlic and sauté for 1-2 minutes until fragrant.
Add the shrimp to the skillet and cook until they turn pink, about 2-3 minutes per side. Remove the shrimp from the skillet and set aside.
Pour the heavy cream into the skillet, stirring to combine with the garlic and butter.
Gradually whisk in the grated Parmesan cheese until the sauce is smooth and creamy.
Season the Alfredo sauce with salt, pepper, and red pepper flakes (if using). Adjust the seasoning to your taste.
Add the blanched broccoli, cooked fettuccine pasta, and cooked shrimp to the skillet. Toss everything together until the pasta and broccoli are coated in the Alfredo sauce.
Garnish with chopped fresh parsley.
Serve the Shrimp and Broccoli Alfredo hot, with lemon wedges on the side.
Allow any leftovers to cool before transferring to freezer-safe containers.

This Shrimp and Broccoli Alfredo is a delightful pasta dish that can be easily frozen for future meals. Reheat it on the stovetop or in the microwave, and enjoy the creamy goodness!

Mexican Quinoa Casserole

Ingredients:

- 1 cup quinoa, rinsed and drained
- 2 cups vegetable broth
- 1 tablespoon olive oil
- 1 onion, diced
- 2 cloves garlic, minced
- 1 bell pepper, diced (any color)
- 1 zucchini, diced
- 1 can (15 oz) black beans, drained and rinsed
- 1 cup corn kernels (fresh, frozen, or canned)
- 1 can (14 oz) diced tomatoes, drained
- 1 teaspoon ground cumin
- 1 teaspoon chili powder
- 1/2 teaspoon paprika
- Salt and pepper to taste
- 1 cup shredded cheddar cheese
- Fresh cilantro, chopped (for garnish)
- Avocado slices (for serving)
- Lime wedges (for serving)

Instructions:

Preheat the oven to 375°F (190°C). Grease a baking dish with olive oil.

In a medium saucepan, combine quinoa and vegetable broth. Bring to a boil, then reduce heat to low, cover, and simmer for about 15 minutes or until the quinoa is cooked and the liquid is absorbed.

In a large skillet, heat olive oil over medium heat. Add diced onion and sauté until softened.

Add minced garlic, diced bell pepper, and diced zucchini to the skillet. Sauté for an additional 5 minutes until the vegetables are tender.

Stir in black beans, corn, diced tomatoes, ground cumin, chili powder, paprika, salt, and pepper. Cook for another 5 minutes, allowing the flavors to meld.

In a large mixing bowl, combine the cooked quinoa and the vegetable mixture. Mix well.

Transfer the quinoa and vegetable mixture to the prepared baking dish, spreading it out evenly.

Sprinkle shredded cheddar cheese over the top.
Bake in the preheated oven for 20-25 minutes or until the cheese is melted and bubbly.
Remove from the oven and let it cool for a few minutes.
Garnish with chopped fresh cilantro.
Serve the Mexican Quinoa Casserole with avocado slices and lime wedges on the side.
Allow any leftovers to cool before transferring to freezer-safe containers.

This Mexican Quinoa Casserole is a nutritious and flavorful dish that freezes well. Reheat it on the stovetop or in the microwave for a quick and satisfying meal. Enjoy!

Spaghetti Bolognese

Ingredients:

- 1 lb ground beef or a mix of beef and pork
- 1 onion, finely chopped
- 2 carrots, diced
- 2 celery stalks, diced
- 3 cloves garlic, minced
- 1/2 cup red wine (optional)
- 1 can (28 oz) crushed tomatoes
- 1/2 cup tomato paste
- 1 cup beef broth
- 1 teaspoon dried oregano
- 1 teaspoon dried basil
- 1/2 teaspoon dried thyme
- Salt and pepper to taste
- 1/2 cup whole milk or heavy cream
- 1 lb spaghetti
- Grated Parmesan cheese (for serving)
- Fresh basil or parsley, chopped (for garnish)

Instructions:

In a large pot or Dutch oven, brown the ground beef over medium-high heat, breaking it apart with a spoon as it cooks.

Add chopped onion, diced carrots, diced celery, and minced garlic to the pot. Sauté until the vegetables are softened.

Pour in red wine (if using) and let it simmer for a few minutes to cook off the alcohol.

Stir in crushed tomatoes, tomato paste, beef broth, dried oregano, dried basil, dried thyme, salt, and pepper. Mix well.

Bring the mixture to a simmer, then reduce the heat to low. Cover and let it simmer for at least 1 hour, stirring occasionally. The longer it simmers, the more flavorful it becomes.

About 10 minutes before serving, stir in whole milk or heavy cream. This adds richness to the sauce.

While the sauce is simmering, cook the spaghetti according to package instructions. Drain and set aside.
Taste and adjust the seasoning of the Bolognese sauce if necessary.
Serve the Bolognese sauce over the cooked spaghetti.
Garnish with grated Parmesan cheese and chopped fresh basil or parsley.
Allow any leftovers to cool before transferring to freezer-safe containers.

This classic Spaghetti Bolognese is a hearty and satisfying meal that freezes well.

Reheat it on the stovetop or in the microwave for a quick and delicious dinner. Enjoy!

Chicken and Rice Burritos

Ingredients:

For the Chicken and Rice Filling:

- 1 lb boneless, skinless chicken breasts, cooked and shredded
- 2 cups cooked white or brown rice
- 1 can (15 oz) black beans, drained and rinsed
- 1 cup corn kernels (fresh, frozen, or canned)
- 1 cup salsa
- 1 teaspoon ground cumin
- 1 teaspoon chili powder
- Salt and pepper to taste
- 1 cup shredded cheddar cheese
- Fresh cilantro, chopped (for garnish)

For Assembling Burritos:

- Large flour tortillas
- Sour cream
- Diced tomatoes
- Sliced avocado
- Shredded lettuce
- Lime wedges

Instructions:

In a large bowl, combine shredded chicken, cooked rice, black beans, corn, salsa, ground cumin, chili powder, salt, and pepper. Mix well.
Heat the chicken and rice mixture in a skillet over medium heat until warmed through.
Sprinkle shredded cheddar cheese over the mixture and stir until the cheese is melted.
Remove from heat and garnish with chopped fresh cilantro.
Warm the flour tortillas in a dry skillet or microwave.

Assemble the burritos by placing a generous portion of the chicken and rice mixture in the center of each tortilla.
Add desired toppings such as sour cream, diced tomatoes, sliced avocado, shredded lettuce, and a squeeze of lime.
Fold the sides of the tortilla over the filling and then fold the bottom and top to form a burrito.
Repeat with the remaining tortillas and filling.
Serve the Chicken and Rice Burritos immediately.
Allow any leftovers to cool before wrapping in foil and transferring to freezer-safe bags.

These Chicken and Rice Burritos are not only delicious for immediate enjoyment but also freezer-friendly for convenient future meals. Reheat them in the oven or microwave, and enjoy your homemade burritos!

Vegetable and Chickpea Stew

Ingredients:

- 2 tablespoons olive oil
- 1 onion, diced
- 3 cloves garlic, minced
- 2 carrots, peeled and sliced
- 2 celery stalks, sliced
- 1 bell pepper (any color), diced
- 1 zucchini, diced
- 1 can (15 oz) chickpeas, drained and rinsed
- 1 can (14 oz) diced tomatoes
- 4 cups vegetable broth
- 1 teaspoon dried thyme
- 1 teaspoon dried rosemary
- 1 teaspoon paprika
- Salt and pepper to taste
- 2 cups chopped kale or spinach
- Fresh parsley, chopped (for garnish)
- Crusty bread (for serving)

Instructions:

In a large pot, heat olive oil over medium heat. Add diced onion and sauté until softened.
Add minced garlic and sauté for an additional 1-2 minutes until fragrant.
Stir in sliced carrots, sliced celery, diced bell pepper, and diced zucchini. Cook for 5-7 minutes until the vegetables start to soften.
Add chickpeas, diced tomatoes, vegetable broth, dried thyme, dried rosemary, paprika, salt, and pepper. Mix well.
Bring the stew to a simmer, then reduce the heat to low. Cover and let it simmer for about 20-25 minutes until the vegetables are tender.
Taste and adjust the seasoning if necessary.
Stir in chopped kale or spinach and cook for an additional 3-5 minutes until the greens are wilted.
Remove the stew from heat and let it cool for a few minutes.
Garnish with chopped fresh parsley.
Serve the Vegetable and Chickpea Stew in bowls, accompanied by crusty bread.

Allow any leftovers to cool before transferring to freezer-safe containers.

This hearty Vegetable and Chickpea Stew is a nutritious and freezer-friendly option. Reheat it on the stovetop for a quick and comforting meal. Enjoy!

Taco Soup

Ingredients:

- 1 lb ground beef or turkey
- 1 onion, diced
- 3 cloves garlic, minced
- 1 bell pepper (any color), diced
- 1 can (15 oz) black beans, drained and rinsed
- 1 can (15 oz) kidney beans, drained and rinsed
- 1 can (15 oz) corn kernels, drained
- 1 can (14 oz) diced tomatoes
- 1 can (4 oz) diced green chilies
- 1 packet taco seasoning mix
- 4 cups beef or vegetable broth
- Salt and pepper to taste
- Tortilla chips (for serving)
- Shredded cheddar cheese (for garnish)
- Sour cream (for garnish)
- Fresh cilantro, chopped (for garnish)
- Lime wedges (for serving)

Instructions:

In a large pot, cook the ground beef or turkey over medium heat until browned. Drain excess fat if needed.
Add diced onion, minced garlic, and diced bell pepper to the pot. Sauté until the vegetables are softened.
Stir in black beans, kidney beans, corn, diced tomatoes, diced green chilies, and taco seasoning mix. Mix well.
Pour in the beef or vegetable broth. Bring the soup to a simmer.
Season with salt and pepper to taste. Simmer for 15-20 minutes to allow the flavors to meld.
Taste and adjust the seasoning if necessary.
Serve the Taco Soup hot.
Garnish with crushed tortilla chips, shredded cheddar cheese, a dollop of sour cream, and chopped fresh cilantro.
Serve lime wedges on the side for squeezing over the soup.

Allow any leftovers to cool before transferring to freezer-safe containers.

This Taco Soup is a flavorful and satisfying dish that freezes well for future meals. Reheat it on the stovetop or in the microwave, and enjoy the delicious taco-inspired flavors!

Mushroom and Spinach Stuffed Shells

Ingredients:

For the Stuffed Shells:

- 1 box (12 oz) jumbo pasta shells
- 2 tablespoons olive oil
- 1 onion, finely chopped
- 3 cloves garlic, minced
- 8 oz mushrooms, finely chopped
- 4 cups fresh spinach, chopped
- 1 cup ricotta cheese
- 1 cup shredded mozzarella cheese
- 1/2 cup grated Parmesan cheese
- 1 large egg
- Salt and pepper to taste

For the Marinara Sauce:

- 1 can (28 oz) crushed tomatoes
- 2 cloves garlic, minced
- 1 teaspoon dried oregano
- 1 teaspoon dried basil
- Salt and pepper to taste

For Assembly:

- 1 cup shredded mozzarella cheese
- Fresh basil or parsley, chopped (for garnish)

Instructions:

Cook the Pasta Shells:
- Cook the jumbo pasta shells according to package instructions. Drain and set aside.

Prepare the Marinara Sauce:

- In a saucepan, combine crushed tomatoes, minced garlic, dried oregano, dried basil, salt, and pepper. Simmer over low heat for about 15-20 minutes, stirring occasionally.

Make the Stuffed Shells Filling:
- In a large skillet, heat olive oil over medium heat. Add chopped onion and sauté until softened.
- Add minced garlic, finely chopped mushrooms, and chopped fresh spinach to the skillet. Sauté until the mushrooms release their moisture, and the spinach wilts. Allow any excess liquid to evaporate.
- In a large bowl, combine ricotta cheese, shredded mozzarella cheese, grated Parmesan cheese, and a beaten egg. Add the sautéed mushroom and spinach mixture. Season with salt and pepper. Mix well.

Assemble the Stuffed Shells:
- Preheat the oven to 375°F (190°C).
- Spread a layer of marinara sauce on the bottom of a baking dish.
- Stuff each cooked pasta shell with a generous spoonful of the mushroom and spinach filling. Place the stuffed shells in the baking dish.
- Pour the remaining marinara sauce over the stuffed shells.
- Sprinkle shredded mozzarella cheese over the top.

Bake:
- Cover the baking dish with aluminum foil and bake in the preheated oven for 25-30 minutes.
- Remove the foil and bake for an additional 10-15 minutes or until the cheese is melted and bubbly, and the edges are golden brown.

Serve:
- Garnish with chopped fresh basil or parsley before serving.

Freezing:
- Allow any leftovers to cool before transferring to freezer-safe containers.

These Mushroom and Spinach Stuffed Shells are a delightful and freezer-friendly dish.

Reheat them in the oven for a delicious and convenient meal. Enjoy!

Orange Ginger Glazed Chicken

Ingredients:

- 4 boneless, skinless chicken breasts
- Salt and black pepper to taste
- 1 cup orange juice
- Zest of 1 orange
- 2 tablespoons soy sauce
- 2 tablespoons honey
- 1 tablespoon fresh ginger, grated
- 2 cloves garlic, minced
- 1 tablespoon cornstarch (optional, for thickening)
- 2 tablespoons green onions, chopped (for garnish)
- Sesame seeds (for garnish)
- Cooked rice or steamed vegetables (for serving)

Instructions:

Prepare the Chicken:
- Season the chicken breasts with salt and black pepper.

Make the Glaze:
- In a bowl, whisk together orange juice, orange zest, soy sauce, honey, grated ginger, and minced garlic.

Cook the Chicken:
- In a large skillet or pan, heat olive oil over medium-high heat.
- Add the chicken breasts and cook for about 6-7 minutes per side or until they are golden brown and cooked through.

Glaze the Chicken:
- Pour the orange-ginger glaze over the cooked chicken in the skillet.
- Allow the glaze to simmer and coat the chicken for an additional 2-3 minutes. You can also spoon the glaze over the chicken to ensure it's well coated.

Thicken the Sauce (Optional):
- If you prefer a thicker sauce, mix cornstarch with a tablespoon of water to create a slurry. Stir the slurry into the glaze and cook for an additional 1-2 minutes until it thickens.

Serve:
- Transfer the glazed chicken to a serving platter.

- Garnish with chopped green onions and sesame seeds.
- Serve the Orange Ginger Glazed Chicken over cooked rice or with steamed vegetables.

Enjoy:
- Allow any leftovers to cool before transferring to freezer-safe containers.

This Orange Ginger Glazed Chicken is a flavorful and zesty dish that freezes well. Reheat it on the stovetop or in the microwave for a quick and tasty meal. Enjoy!

Cauliflower Fried Rice

Ingredients:

- 1 medium head cauliflower, grated or processed into rice-sized pieces
- 2 tablespoons vegetable oil
- 1 onion, finely chopped
- 2 carrots, diced
- 1 cup frozen peas
- 2 cloves garlic, minced
- 2 eggs, beaten
- 3 tablespoons soy sauce
- 1 tablespoon sesame oil
- 1 teaspoon ginger, grated
- 2 green onions, sliced (for garnish)
- Sesame seeds (for garnish)

Instructions:

Prepare the Cauliflower Rice:
- Remove the leaves and stem from the cauliflower. Grate the cauliflower using a box grater or process it in a food processor until it resembles rice-sized pieces.

Stir-Fry Vegetables:
- Heat vegetable oil in a large skillet or wok over medium-high heat.
- Add chopped onions and diced carrots. Stir-fry for 3-4 minutes until the vegetables begin to soften.
- Add frozen peas and minced garlic. Continue to stir-fry for an additional 2-3 minutes.

Cook the Cauliflower Rice:
- Push the vegetables to the side of the pan and add the grated cauliflower.
- Stir the cauliflower rice into the vegetables, combining them well. Cook for about 5-7 minutes until the cauliflower is tender but not mushy.

Scramble the Eggs:
- Push the cauliflower and vegetables to one side of the pan. Pour beaten eggs into the empty side.
- Scramble the eggs and cook until they are fully cooked.

Combine and Season:

- Mix the scrambled eggs with the cauliflower rice and vegetables.
- Drizzle soy sauce and sesame oil over the mixture.
- Add grated ginger and stir everything together until well combined.

Garnish and Serve:
- Garnish with sliced green onions and sesame seeds.
- Taste and adjust the seasoning, adding more soy sauce or sesame oil if desired.
- Serve the Cauliflower Fried Rice hot.

Freezing:
- Allow any leftovers to cool before transferring to freezer-safe containers.

This Cauliflower Fried Rice is a healthy and delicious alternative to traditional fried rice.

Reheat it on the stovetop or in the microwave for a quick and satisfying meal. Enjoy!

Beef and Black Bean Enchiladas

Ingredients:

For the Filling:

- 1 lb ground beef
- 1 onion, finely chopped
- 2 cloves garlic, minced
- 1 can (15 oz) black beans, drained and rinsed
- 1 cup corn kernels (fresh, frozen, or canned)
- 1 teaspoon ground cumin
- 1 teaspoon chili powder
- Salt and pepper to taste
- 1 cup shredded cheddar cheese

For the Enchilada Sauce:

- 2 tablespoons vegetable oil
- 2 tablespoons all-purpose flour
- 3 tablespoons chili powder
- 1 teaspoon ground cumin
- 1/2 teaspoon garlic powder
- 1/2 teaspoon onion powder
- 1/4 teaspoon cayenne pepper (optional, for heat)
- 1 can (15 oz) tomato sauce
- 1 cup chicken broth
- Salt and pepper to taste

For Assembly:

- 10-12 small flour tortillas
- 1 cup shredded Monterey Jack cheese
- Fresh cilantro, chopped (for garnish)
- Sour cream (for serving)
- Sliced green onions (for garnish)
- Salsa or diced tomatoes (for serving)

Instructions:

Cook the Filling:
- In a large skillet, cook ground beef over medium-high heat until browned. Drain excess fat if needed.
- Add chopped onion and minced garlic to the skillet. Sauté until the onion is softened.
- Stir in black beans, corn, ground cumin, chili powder, salt, and pepper. Cook for an additional 3-5 minutes until the mixture is well combined.
- Remove from heat and let it cool slightly. Stir in shredded cheddar cheese.

Prepare the Enchilada Sauce:
- In a saucepan, heat vegetable oil over medium heat. Stir in flour and cook for 1-2 minutes to create a roux.
- Add chili powder, ground cumin, garlic powder, onion powder, and cayenne pepper (if using). Mix well.
- Gradually whisk in tomato sauce and chicken broth. Bring the mixture to a simmer, stirring constantly.
- Cook for 5-7 minutes until the sauce thickens. Season with salt and pepper to taste.

Assemble the Enchiladas:
- Preheat the oven to 375°F (190°C).
- Spread a thin layer of enchilada sauce on the bottom of a baking dish.
- Warm the flour tortillas in the microwave or on a skillet.
- Spoon the beef and black bean filling onto each tortilla. Roll them up and place them seam-side down in the baking dish.
- Pour the remaining enchilada sauce over the rolled tortillas.
- Sprinkle shredded Monterey Jack cheese over the top.

Bake:
- Bake in the preheated oven for 20-25 minutes or until the cheese is melted and bubbly.

Serve:
- Garnish with chopped fresh cilantro and sliced green onions.
- Serve the Beef and Black Bean Enchiladas with sour cream and salsa or diced tomatoes on the side.

Freezing:
- Allow any leftovers to cool before transferring to freezer-safe containers.

These Beef and Black Bean Enchiladas are a flavorful and freezer-friendly option. Reheat them in the oven for a delicious and convenient meal. Enjoy!

Creamy Pesto Chicken Pasta

Ingredients:

- 8 oz fettuccine or your favorite pasta
- 1 lb boneless, skinless chicken breasts, thinly sliced
- Salt and black pepper to taste
- 2 tablespoons olive oil
- 3 cloves garlic, minced
- 1 cup cherry tomatoes, halved
- 1/2 cup sun-dried tomatoes, chopped
- 1 cup fresh spinach leaves
- 1/2 cup basil pesto (store-bought or homemade)
- 1 cup heavy cream
- 1/2 cup grated Parmesan cheese
- Red pepper flakes (optional, for heat)
- Fresh basil, chopped (for garnish)

Instructions:

Cook the Pasta:
- Cook the fettuccine or pasta according to package instructions. Drain and set aside.

Season and Cook the Chicken:
- Season the chicken slices with salt and black pepper.
- In a large skillet, heat olive oil over medium-high heat. Add the sliced chicken and cook until browned and cooked through, about 4-5 minutes per side. Remove the chicken from the skillet and set aside.

Prepare the Sauce:
- In the same skillet, add minced garlic and sauté for 1-2 minutes until fragrant.
- Add cherry tomatoes, sun-dried tomatoes, and fresh spinach to the skillet. Cook until the spinach wilts and the tomatoes are softened.
- Stir in basil pesto and heavy cream. Mix well.
- Add grated Parmesan cheese and stir until the cheese is melted and the sauce is creamy.

Combine and Serve:

- Add the cooked chicken back to the skillet, stirring to coat it with the creamy pesto sauce.
- Toss in the cooked pasta and mix until everything is well combined.
- Season with red pepper flakes if you like a bit of heat.

Garnish and Enjoy:
- Garnish with chopped fresh basil.
- Serve the Creamy Pesto Chicken Pasta hot.

Freezing:
- Allow any leftovers to cool before transferring to freezer-safe containers.

This Creamy Pesto Chicken Pasta is a delightful and freezer-friendly dish. Reheat it on the stovetop or in the microwave for a quick and satisfying meal. Enjoy!

Butternut Squash Soup

Ingredients:

- 1 large butternut squash, peeled, seeded, and diced
- 1 onion, chopped
- 2 carrots, peeled and chopped
- 2 apples, peeled, cored, and chopped
- 3 cloves garlic, minced
- 4 cups vegetable or chicken broth
- 1 teaspoon ground cinnamon
- 1/2 teaspoon ground nutmeg
- 1/2 teaspoon ground ginger
- Salt and pepper to taste
- 2 tablespoons olive oil
- 1 cup coconut milk or heavy cream (optional)
- Toasted pumpkin seeds or croutons (for garnish)

Instructions:

Prepare the Vegetables:
- Peel, seed, and dice the butternut squash. Chop the onion, peel and chop the carrots, peel, core, and chop the apples, and mince the garlic.

Sauté Vegetables:
- In a large pot, heat olive oil over medium heat. Add chopped onion and sauté until softened.
- Add minced garlic and sauté for an additional 1-2 minutes until fragrant.
- Add chopped butternut squash, carrots, and apples to the pot. Cook for about 5 minutes, stirring occasionally.

Season and Simmer:
- Pour in the vegetable or chicken broth.
- Add ground cinnamon, ground nutmeg, ground ginger, salt, and pepper. Stir well.
- Bring the mixture to a boil, then reduce the heat to low. Cover and simmer for about 20-25 minutes or until the vegetables are tender.

Blend the Soup:

- Use an immersion blender to blend the soup until smooth. Alternatively, transfer the soup in batches to a blender and blend until smooth. Be cautious when blending hot liquids.

Finish the Soup:
- Stir in coconut milk or heavy cream if using. Adjust the consistency with additional broth if needed.
- Taste and adjust the seasoning.

Serve:
- Ladle the butternut squash soup into bowls.
- Garnish with toasted pumpkin seeds or croutons.
- Serve the soup hot.

Freezing:
- Allow any leftovers to cool before transferring to freezer-safe containers.

This Butternut Squash Soup is a comforting and flavorful dish that freezes well. Reheat it on the stovetop for a quick and satisfying meal. Enjoy!

Salmon and Asparagus Foil Packets

Ingredients:

- 4 salmon fillets
- 1 bunch asparagus, trimmed
- 4 tablespoons olive oil
- 4 cloves garlic, minced
- 2 tablespoons fresh lemon juice
- 1 teaspoon lemon zest
- 1 teaspoon dried thyme
- Salt and black pepper to taste
- 1 tablespoon fresh dill, chopped (optional, for garnish)
- Lemon slices (for garnish)

Instructions:

Preheat the Oven:
- Preheat your oven to 400°F (200°C).

Prepare Foil Packets:
- Cut four large pieces of aluminum foil.
- Place a salmon fillet in the center of each piece of foil.
- Divide the trimmed asparagus evenly among the foil packets, arranging them next to the salmon.

Make the Marinade:
- In a small bowl, whisk together olive oil, minced garlic, lemon juice, lemon zest, dried thyme, salt, and black pepper.

Drizzle and Seal:
- Drizzle the marinade over each salmon fillet and asparagus.
- Seal the foil packets by folding the edges over and crimping them to create a tight seal.

Bake:
- Place the foil packets on a baking sheet and bake in the preheated oven for 15-20 minutes or until the salmon is cooked through and flakes easily with a fork.

Garnish and Serve:
- Carefully open the foil packets, being cautious of the hot steam.
- Garnish the salmon and asparagus with fresh dill and lemon slices.
- Serve the Salmon and Asparagus Foil Packets immediately.

Freezing:
- Allow any leftovers to cool before transferring to freezer-safe containers.

These Salmon and Asparagus Foil Packets are not only easy to make but also a convenient freezer-friendly option. Reheat them in the oven for a quick and delicious meal. Enjoy!

Vegetarian Enchilada Casserole

Ingredients:

For the Enchilada Sauce:

- 2 tablespoons vegetable oil
- 2 tablespoons all-purpose flour
- 3 tablespoons chili powder
- 1 teaspoon ground cumin
- 1/2 teaspoon garlic powder
- 1/2 teaspoon onion powder
- 1/4 teaspoon cayenne pepper (optional, for heat)
- 1 can (15 oz) tomato sauce
- 1 cup vegetable broth
- Salt and pepper to taste

For the Filling:

- 1 tablespoon vegetable oil
- 1 onion, chopped
- 1 bell pepper (any color), chopped
- 1 zucchini, diced
- 1 can (15 oz) black beans, drained and rinsed
- 1 cup corn kernels (fresh, frozen, or canned)
- 1 teaspoon ground cumin
- 1 teaspoon chili powder
- Salt and pepper to taste

Other Ingredients:

- 12 small corn tortillas
- 2 cups shredded cheese (cheddar, Monterey Jack, or a blend)
- Fresh cilantro, chopped (for garnish)
- Sour cream (for serving)
- Sliced green onions (for garnish)
- Avocado slices (for serving)

Instructions:

Prepare the Enchilada Sauce:
- In a saucepan, heat vegetable oil over medium heat. Stir in flour and cook for 1-2 minutes to create a roux.
- Add chili powder, ground cumin, garlic powder, onion powder, and cayenne pepper (if using). Mix well.
- Gradually whisk in tomato sauce and vegetable broth. Bring the mixture to a simmer, stirring constantly.
- Cook for 5-7 minutes until the sauce thickens. Season with salt and pepper to taste.

Prepare the Filling:
- In a skillet, heat vegetable oil over medium-high heat.
- Add chopped onion, bell pepper, and diced zucchini. Sauté until the vegetables are softened.
- Stir in black beans, corn, ground cumin, chili powder, salt, and pepper. Cook for an additional 3-5 minutes until the mixture is well combined.

Assemble the Casserole:
- Preheat the oven to 375°F (190°C).
- Spread a thin layer of enchilada sauce in the bottom of a baking dish.
- Dip each corn tortilla in the enchilada sauce to coat it lightly.
- Place a portion of the vegetable filling in the center of each tortilla. Roll up and place seam-side down in the baking dish.
- Pour the remaining enchilada sauce over the rolled tortillas.
- Sprinkle shredded cheese over the top.

Bake:
- Bake in the preheated oven for 20-25 minutes or until the cheese is melted and bubbly.

Garnish and Serve:
- Garnish with chopped fresh cilantro and sliced green onions.
- Serve the Vegetarian Enchilada Casserole hot, with sour cream and avocado slices on the side.

Freezing:
- Allow any leftovers to cool before transferring to freezer-safe containers.

This Vegetarian Enchilada Casserole is a flavorful and freezer-friendly dish. Reheat it in the oven for a convenient and delicious meal. Enjoy!

Sesame Ginger Beef Stir-Fry

Ingredients:

For the Marinade:

- 1 lb flank steak, thinly sliced
- 3 tablespoons soy sauce
- 1 tablespoon rice vinegar
- 1 tablespoon sesame oil
- 1 tablespoon honey
- 2 teaspoons fresh ginger, grated
- 2 cloves garlic, minced
- 1 tablespoon cornstarch

For the Stir-Fry:

- 2 tablespoons vegetable oil
- 1 bell pepper, thinly sliced
- 1 carrot, julienned
- 1 cup broccoli florets
- 1 cup snap peas, trimmed
- 2 green onions, sliced
- Sesame seeds (for garnish)

For Serving:

- Cooked rice or noodles

Instructions:

Marinate the Beef:
- In a bowl, combine sliced flank steak with soy sauce, rice vinegar, sesame oil, honey, grated ginger, minced garlic, and cornstarch. Mix well to coat the beef evenly. Allow it to marinate for at least 15-20 minutes.

Prepare the Vegetables:

- While the beef is marinating, prepare the vegetables by slicing the bell pepper, julienned carrot, broccoli florets, and trimming the snap peas.

Stir-Fry:
- Heat vegetable oil in a wok or large skillet over high heat.
- Add the marinated beef and stir-fry for 2-3 minutes until browned and cooked through. Remove the beef from the wok and set aside.
- In the same wok, add a bit more oil if needed. Stir-fry the bell pepper, julienned carrot, broccoli florets, and snap peas for 3-4 minutes or until the vegetables are crisp-tender.

Combine and Finish:
- Return the cooked beef to the wok with the vegetables.
- Add sliced green onions and toss everything together for an additional 1-2 minutes.
- Taste and adjust the seasoning if necessary.

Serve:
- Serve the Sesame Ginger Beef Stir-Fry over cooked rice or noodles.
- Garnish with sesame seeds.

Enjoy:
- This stir-fry is best enjoyed immediately.

Freezing:
- If you plan to freeze, allow the stir-fry to cool before transferring to freezer-safe containers.

This Sesame Ginger Beef Stir-Fry is a quick and flavorful dish perfect for a weeknight dinner. Reheat it on the stovetop for a convenient and delicious meal. Enjoy!

Chicken and Broccoli Bake

Ingredients:

- 2 boneless, skinless chicken breasts, cooked and shredded
- 4 cups broccoli florets, blanched
- 1 cup shredded cheddar cheese
- 1/2 cup mayonnaise
- 1/2 cup sour cream
- 1 tablespoon Dijon mustard
- 1 teaspoon garlic powder
- Salt and black pepper to taste
- 1 cup crushed butter crackers (such as Ritz)
- 2 tablespoons melted butter
- Fresh parsley, chopped (for garnish)

Instructions:

Preheat the Oven:
- Preheat your oven to 375°F (190°C). Grease a baking dish.

Prepare Chicken and Broccoli:
- Cook the chicken breasts (grill, bake, or poach) until fully cooked. Shred the chicken using two forks.
- Blanch the broccoli florets in boiling water for 2 minutes. Drain and set aside.

Make the Sauce:
- In a bowl, combine shredded chicken, blanched broccoli, shredded cheddar cheese, mayonnaise, sour cream, Dijon mustard, garlic powder, salt, and black pepper. Mix well to coat the chicken and broccoli evenly.

Assemble the Bake:
- Transfer the chicken and broccoli mixture to the prepared baking dish, spreading it evenly.

Prepare the Topping:
- In a small bowl, mix crushed butter crackers with melted butter.

Top and Bake:
- Sprinkle the buttered cracker mixture over the chicken and broccoli.
- Bake in the preheated oven for 20-25 minutes or until the top is golden brown, and the bake is heated through.

Garnish and Serve:
- Remove from the oven and let it cool for a few minutes.
- Garnish with chopped fresh parsley.
- Serve the Chicken and Broccoli Bake warm.

Freezing:
- Allow any leftovers to cool before transferring to freezer-safe containers.

This Chicken and Broccoli Bake is a comforting casserole that freezes well. Reheat it in the oven for a quick and satisfying meal. Enjoy!

Mediterranean Quinoa Salad

Ingredients:

- 1 cup quinoa, rinsed and cooked according to package instructions
- 1 cup cherry tomatoes, halved
- 1 cucumber, diced
- 1 cup Kalamata olives, pitted and sliced
- 1/2 cup red onion, finely chopped
- 1/2 cup feta cheese, crumbled
- 1/2 cup fresh parsley, chopped
- 1/4 cup fresh mint, chopped
- 1/4 cup extra-virgin olive oil
- 2 tablespoons red wine vinegar
- 1 teaspoon dried oregano
- Salt and black pepper to taste
- Lemon wedges (for serving)

Instructions:

Cook Quinoa:
- Rinse the quinoa under cold water. Cook the quinoa according to the package instructions. Once cooked, fluff it with a fork and let it cool.

Prepare Vegetables:
- In a large bowl, combine the cooked quinoa, halved cherry tomatoes, diced cucumber, sliced Kalamata olives, chopped red onion, crumbled feta cheese, chopped fresh parsley, and chopped fresh mint.

Make the Dressing:
- In a small bowl, whisk together extra-virgin olive oil, red wine vinegar, dried oregano, salt, and black pepper.

Combine and Toss:
- Pour the dressing over the quinoa and vegetable mixture.
- Toss everything together until well combined and evenly coated with the dressing.

Chill and Serve:
- Cover the bowl and refrigerate the Mediterranean Quinoa Salad for at least 30 minutes to allow the flavors to meld.
- Before serving, taste and adjust the seasoning if necessary.

Garnish and Serve:
- Garnish the salad with additional fresh herbs if desired.
- Serve the Mediterranean Quinoa Salad chilled, with lemon wedges on the side for squeezing over individual servings.

Enjoy:
- This salad is great as a light meal on its own or as a side dish.

Freezing:
- While this salad is best enjoyed fresh, you can freeze the cooked quinoa separately and combine it with fresh vegetables and dressing after thawing.

This Mediterranean Quinoa Salad is a refreshing and nutritious dish that's perfect for a light lunch or as a side for dinner. Enjoy!

Turkey and Vegetable Chili

Ingredients:

- 1 lb ground turkey
- 1 tablespoon olive oil
- 1 onion, diced
- 2 bell peppers (any color), diced
- 2 carrots, diced
- 3 cloves garlic, minced
- 1 can (15 oz) kidney beans, drained and rinsed
- 1 can (15 oz) black beans, drained and rinsed
- 1 can (15 oz) diced tomatoes
- 1 cup corn kernels (fresh, frozen, or canned)
- 1 cup tomato sauce
- 2 tablespoons tomato paste
- 1 cup chicken or vegetable broth
- 2 teaspoons ground cumin
- 2 teaspoons chili powder
- 1 teaspoon dried oregano
- 1 teaspoon smoked paprika
- Salt and black pepper to taste
- Optional toppings: shredded cheese, sour cream, chopped green onions, cilantro

Instructions:

Cook the Turkey:
- In a large pot or Dutch oven, heat olive oil over medium-high heat. Add ground turkey and cook until browned, breaking it apart with a spoon as it cooks.

Saute Vegetables:
- Add diced onion, bell peppers, carrots, and minced garlic to the pot. Cook for 5-7 minutes until the vegetables are softened.

Add Beans and Tomatoes:
- Stir in kidney beans, black beans, diced tomatoes, and corn.

Season the Chili:

- Add tomato sauce, tomato paste, chicken or vegetable broth, ground cumin, chili powder, dried oregano, smoked paprika, salt, and black pepper. Stir well to combine.

Simmer:
- Bring the chili to a simmer, then reduce the heat to low. Cover and let it simmer for at least 30 minutes to allow the flavors to meld. You can simmer longer for even more flavor.

Adjust Seasoning:
- Taste the chili and adjust the seasoning if needed. Add more salt, pepper, or spices according to your preference.

Serve:
- Ladle the turkey and vegetable chili into bowls.
- Top with shredded cheese, a dollop of sour cream, chopped green onions, or cilantro if desired.

Enjoy:
- Serve the turkey and vegetable chili hot and enjoy a comforting and hearty meal.

Freezing:
- Allow any leftovers to cool before transferring to freezer-safe containers.

This Turkey and Vegetable Chili is a wholesome and freezer-friendly dish. Reheat it on the stovetop for a quick and satisfying meal. Enjoy!

Caprese Stuffed Chicken

Ingredients:

- 4 boneless, skinless chicken breasts
- Salt and black pepper to taste
- 1 teaspoon garlic powder
- 1 teaspoon dried oregano
- 4 slices fresh mozzarella cheese
- 2 large tomatoes, sliced
- 1 bunch fresh basil leaves
- Balsamic glaze (store-bought or homemade)

Instructions:

Preheat the Oven:
- Preheat your oven to 375°F (190°C).

Prepare the Chicken:
- Lay each chicken breast flat on a cutting board. Use a sharp knife to make a horizontal slit in the thickest part of each breast, creating a pocket for the stuffing.
- Season the chicken breasts with salt, black pepper, garlic powder, and dried oregano.

Stuff the Chicken:
- Stuff each chicken breast with a slice of fresh mozzarella, tomato slices, and a few basil leaves. Press the edges of the chicken together to seal the pocket.

Season the Exterior:
- Season the outside of each chicken breast with a bit more salt, black pepper, and dried oregano.

Bake:
- Place the stuffed chicken breasts on a baking sheet or in a baking dish.
- Bake in the preheated oven for 25-30 minutes or until the chicken is cooked through and the juices run clear.

Broil (Optional):
- If you want a golden-brown top, you can broil the chicken for an additional 2-3 minutes at the end of the cooking time.

Drizzle with Balsamic Glaze:

- Remove the stuffed chicken from the oven.
- Drizzle balsamic glaze over each chicken breast.

Serve:
- Serve the Caprese Stuffed Chicken hot.

Enjoy:
- This dish pairs well with a side of roasted vegetables, salad, or pasta.

Freezing:
- Allow any leftovers to cool before transferring to freezer-safe containers.

This Caprese Stuffed Chicken is a delightful and freezer-friendly option. Reheat it on the stovetop or in the oven for a quick and tasty meal. Enjoy!

Honey Mustard Glazed Pork Chops

Ingredients:

- 4 bone-in pork chops
- Salt and black pepper to taste
- 2 tablespoons olive oil

For the Honey Mustard Glaze:

- 1/4 cup Dijon mustard
- 2 tablespoons honey
- 2 tablespoons whole-grain mustard
- 2 cloves garlic, minced
- 1 tablespoon soy sauce
- 1 tablespoon apple cider vinegar
- 1 teaspoon dried thyme (optional)

Instructions:

Preheat the Oven:
- Preheat your oven to 375°F (190°C).

Season the Pork Chops:
- Pat the pork chops dry with paper towels. Season both sides with salt and black pepper.

Sear the Pork Chops:
- In an oven-safe skillet, heat olive oil over medium-high heat. Sear the pork chops for 2-3 minutes on each side until they develop a golden-brown crust.

Prepare the Glaze:
- In a small bowl, whisk together Dijon mustard, honey, whole-grain mustard, minced garlic, soy sauce, apple cider vinegar, and dried thyme (if using).

Glaze the Pork Chops:
- Brush the honey mustard glaze over each pork chop, ensuring an even coating.

Bake:
- Transfer the skillet to the preheated oven.
- Bake for 15-20 minutes or until the internal temperature of the pork chops reaches 145°F (63°C).

Broil (Optional):
- If you want a caramelized top, you can broil the pork chops for an additional 2-3 minutes at the end of the cooking time.

Rest and Serve:
- Remove the pork chops from the oven and let them rest for a few minutes before serving.

Serve:
- Drizzle any remaining glaze over the pork chops.
- Serve the Honey Mustard Glazed Pork Chops hot.

Enjoy:
- These pork chops pair well with sides like roasted vegetables, mashed potatoes, or a green salad.

Freezing:
- Allow any leftovers to cool before transferring to freezer-safe containers.

These Honey Mustard Glazed Pork Chops are a flavorful and freezer-friendly option. Reheat them on the stovetop or in the oven for a quick and delicious meal. Enjoy!

Chicken and Rice Casserole

Ingredients:

- 1 1/2 cups long-grain white rice
- 1 lb boneless, skinless chicken breasts, diced
- 1 tablespoon olive oil
- 1 onion, finely chopped
- 2 carrots, diced
- 2 celery stalks, diced
- 2 cloves garlic, minced
- 1 teaspoon dried thyme
- 1 teaspoon dried rosemary
- Salt and black pepper to taste
- 3 cups chicken broth
- 1 cup frozen peas
- 1 cup shredded cheddar cheese
- 1/2 cup grated Parmesan cheese
- Fresh parsley, chopped (for garnish)

Instructions:

Preheat the Oven:
- Preheat your oven to 375°F (190°C).

Cook the Rice:
- Cook the white rice according to package instructions. Set aside.

Cook Chicken:
- In a large oven-safe skillet or a separate pan, heat olive oil over medium-high heat.
- Add diced chicken and cook until browned on all sides. Remove the chicken from the pan and set aside.

Sauté Vegetables:
- In the same skillet, add chopped onion, carrots, celery, and minced garlic. Sauté until the vegetables are softened.

Add Herbs and Seasoning:
- Stir in dried thyme, dried rosemary, salt, and black pepper.

Combine Rice and Chicken:
- Add the cooked rice and browned chicken back to the skillet. Mix well with the sautéed vegetables.

Pour Chicken Broth:
- Pour chicken broth over the rice and chicken mixture. Stir to combine.

Add Peas and Cheese:
- Mix in frozen peas, shredded cheddar cheese, and grated Parmesan cheese.

Bake:
- Cover the skillet with a lid or aluminum foil.
- Bake in the preheated oven for 25-30 minutes or until the rice is cooked, and the liquid is absorbed.

Broil (Optional):
- If you want a golden-brown top, you can broil the casserole for an additional 2-3 minutes at the end of the cooking time.

Garnish and Serve:
- Remove from the oven and let it rest for a few minutes.
- Garnish with chopped fresh parsley.
- Serve the Chicken and Rice Casserole hot.

Enjoy:
- This casserole makes for a complete and comforting meal.

Freezing:
- Allow any leftovers to cool before transferring to freezer-safe containers.

This Chicken and Rice Casserole is a hearty and freezer-friendly dish. Reheat it on the stovetop or in the oven for a convenient and delicious meal. Enjoy!

Vegetable and Lentil Curry

Ingredients:

- 1 cup dry lentils (red or green), rinsed and drained
- 2 tablespoons vegetable oil
- 1 large onion, finely chopped
- 3 cloves garlic, minced
- 1 tablespoon fresh ginger, grated
- 1 bell pepper, diced
- 2 carrots, diced
- 1 zucchini, diced
- 1 can (14 oz) diced tomatoes
- 1 can (14 oz) coconut milk
- 2 tablespoons curry powder
- 1 teaspoon ground cumin
- 1 teaspoon ground coriander
- 1/2 teaspoon turmeric powder
- 1/2 teaspoon chili powder (adjust to taste)
- Salt and black pepper to taste
- Fresh cilantro, chopped (for garnish)
- Cooked rice or naan (for serving)

Instructions:

Prepare Lentils:
- In a pot, combine the rinsed lentils with enough water to cover them. Bring to a boil, then reduce the heat and simmer for about 15-20 minutes or until the lentils are tender but not mushy. Drain any excess water and set aside.

Sauté Aromatics:
- In a large skillet or pot, heat vegetable oil over medium heat. Add chopped onions, minced garlic, and grated ginger. Sauté until the onions are translucent and fragrant.

Add Vegetables:
- Add diced bell pepper, carrots, and zucchini to the skillet. Cook for 5-7 minutes until the vegetables begin to soften.

Spice it Up:

- Stir in curry powder, ground cumin, ground coriander, turmeric powder, and chili powder. Cook for an additional 1-2 minutes to toast the spices.

Combine Lentils and Tomatoes:
- Add the cooked lentils to the skillet, followed by diced tomatoes (with their juices). Mix well to combine.

Pour Coconut Milk:
- Pour in coconut milk, stirring to create a creamy curry base.

Simmer:
- Bring the curry to a gentle simmer. Let it cook for 15-20 minutes to allow the flavors to meld and the vegetables to become tender.

Season and Garnish:
- Season the curry with salt and black pepper according to your taste.
- Garnish with freshly chopped cilantro.

Serve:
- Serve the Vegetable and Lentil Curry over cooked rice or with naan bread.

Enjoy:
- This curry is flavorful, nutritious, and perfect for a satisfying vegetarian meal.

Freezing:
- Allow any leftovers to cool before transferring to freezer-safe containers.

This Vegetable and Lentil Curry is a delicious and freezer-friendly option. Reheat it on the stovetop for a quick and flavorful meal. Enjoy!

Cilantro Lime Shrimp

Ingredients:

- 1 lb large shrimp, peeled and deveined
- 2 tablespoons olive oil
- 4 cloves garlic, minced
- 1/4 cup fresh cilantro, chopped
- Zest of 1 lime
- Juice of 2 limes
- 1 teaspoon ground cumin
- 1/2 teaspoon chili powder
- Salt and black pepper to taste
- Lime wedges (for serving)
- Chopped fresh cilantro (for garnish)

Instructions:

Marinate the Shrimp:
- In a bowl, combine shrimp with olive oil, minced garlic, chopped cilantro, lime zest, lime juice, ground cumin, chili powder, salt, and black pepper. Toss to coat the shrimp evenly. Allow them to marinate for at least 15-20 minutes.

Cook the Shrimp:
- Heat a large skillet over medium-high heat. Add the marinated shrimp to the skillet in a single layer.
- Cook for 2-3 minutes per side or until the shrimp turn pink and opaque.

Garnish and Serve:
- Remove the skillet from heat.
- Garnish the Cilantro Lime Shrimp with additional chopped cilantro.
- Serve hot with lime wedges on the side for squeezing.

Serve:
- This dish is delicious on its own, over rice, or as a filling for tacos.

Enjoy:
- The combination of cilantro and lime adds a refreshing and zesty flavor to the succulent shrimp.

Freezing (Optional):
- If you have leftovers, allow the shrimp to cool before transferring them to freezer-safe containers.

This Cilantro Lime Shrimp is a quick, flavorful dish that can be served as a main course or used in various recipes. Reheat it on the stovetop for a fast and tasty meal. Enjoy!

Greek Chicken Souvlaki

Ingredients:

For the Chicken Marinade:

- 1.5 lbs boneless, skinless chicken breasts, cut into cubes
- 1/4 cup olive oil
- 3 tablespoons Greek yogurt
- 3 cloves garlic, minced
- 1 teaspoon dried oregano
- 1 teaspoon dried thyme
- Zest of 1 lemon
- Juice of 1 lemon
- Salt and black pepper to taste

For the Tzatziki Sauce:

- 1 cup Greek yogurt
- 1/2 cucumber, finely grated and drained
- 2 cloves garlic, minced
- 1 tablespoon fresh dill, chopped
- 1 tablespoon extra-virgin olive oil
- Salt and black pepper to taste

For Serving:

- Pita bread
- Cherry tomatoes, halved
- Red onion, thinly sliced
- Cucumber, sliced
- Feta cheese, crumbled
- Fresh parsley, chopped

Instructions:

Marinate the Chicken:
- In a bowl, combine olive oil, Greek yogurt, minced garlic, dried oregano, dried thyme, lemon zest, lemon juice, salt, and black pepper.

- Add the chicken cubes to the marinade, ensuring they are well-coated. Cover and refrigerate for at least 1-2 hours, or overnight for the best flavor.

Prepare Tzatziki Sauce:
- In a separate bowl, mix Greek yogurt, finely grated cucumber (make sure to drain excess liquid), minced garlic, chopped fresh dill, olive oil, salt, and black pepper. Stir well to combine. Refrigerate until ready to serve.

Skewer and Grill:
- Preheat the grill or grill pan over medium-high heat.
- Thread the marinated chicken cubes onto skewers.
- Grill the chicken skewers for about 6-8 minutes, turning occasionally, until the chicken is fully cooked and has a nice char.

Warm Pita Bread:
- Warm the pita bread on the grill for about 1-2 minutes per side.

Serve:
- Serve the Greek Chicken Souvlaki on warm pita bread.
- Top with cherry tomatoes, sliced red onion, cucumber slices, crumbled feta cheese, and a drizzle of tzatziki sauce.
- Garnish with chopped fresh parsley.

Enjoy:
- This Greek Chicken Souvlaki is a delicious and satisfying meal.

Freezing (Optional):
- If you have leftover marinated chicken, you can freeze it in airtight containers. Thaw before grilling.

This Greek Chicken Souvlaki is a flavorful and freezer-friendly dish. Reheat or finish cooking on the grill for a quick and tasty meal. Enjoy!

Macaroni and Cheese with Broccoli

Ingredients:

- 2 cups elbow macaroni (or pasta of your choice)
- 2 cups broccoli florets
- 1/4 cup unsalted butter
- 1/4 cup all-purpose flour
- 2 cups whole milk
- 2 cups sharp cheddar cheese, shredded
- 1/2 cup Parmesan cheese, grated
- 1 teaspoon Dijon mustard
- Salt and black pepper to taste
- 1/2 teaspoon garlic powder (optional)
- 1/4 teaspoon nutmeg (optional)
- Bread crumbs (optional, for topping)

Instructions:

Cook the Pasta and Broccoli:
- Cook the elbow macaroni according to the package instructions. In the last 2-3 minutes of cooking, add the broccoli florets to the boiling water. Drain the pasta and broccoli and set aside.

Make the Cheese Sauce:
- In a large saucepan, melt the butter over medium heat. Add the flour and whisk continuously to create a roux. Cook for 1-2 minutes, stirring constantly.
- Gradually pour in the milk, whisking constantly to avoid lumps. Cook until the mixture thickens.

Add Cheese and Seasoning:
- Reduce the heat to low. Add shredded cheddar cheese and Parmesan cheese to the sauce. Stir until the cheese is melted and the sauce is smooth.
- Stir in Dijon mustard, salt, black pepper, garlic powder (if using), and nutmeg (if using). Adjust the seasoning to taste.

Combine Pasta and Sauce:
- Add the cooked pasta and broccoli to the cheese sauce. Stir until the pasta and broccoli are well coated with the cheese sauce.

Optional Topping:
- If desired, transfer the macaroni and cheese with broccoli to a baking dish and sprinkle with bread crumbs for a crunchy topping.

Serve:
- Serve the Macaroni and Cheese with Broccoli hot.

Enjoy:
- This dish is a comforting and hearty meal that combines the creaminess of the cheese sauce with the freshness of broccoli.

Freezing (Optional):
- Allow any leftovers to cool before transferring to freezer-safe containers.

This Macaroni and Cheese with Broccoli is a classic comfort food with a nutritious twist. Reheat it in the oven or on the stovetop for a quick and satisfying meal. Enjoy!

Asian Peanut Noodles with Tofu

Ingredients:

For the Peanut Sauce:

- 1/3 cup creamy peanut butter
- 3 tablespoons soy sauce
- 2 tablespoons rice vinegar
- 2 tablespoons sesame oil
- 1 tablespoon honey
- 1 tablespoon fresh ginger, grated
- 2 cloves garlic, minced
- Red pepper flakes (optional, for heat)

For the Noodles and Tofu:

- 8 oz rice noodles or any noodles of your choice
- 1 block extra-firm tofu, pressed and cubed
- 2 tablespoons vegetable oil
- 1 bell pepper, thinly sliced
- 1 carrot, julienned
- 1 cup snow peas, ends trimmed
- Green onions, sliced (for garnish)
- Sesame seeds (for garnish)

Instructions:

Prepare the Peanut Sauce:
- In a bowl, whisk together peanut butter, soy sauce, rice vinegar, sesame oil, honey, grated ginger, minced garlic, and red pepper flakes (if using). Set aside.

Cook the Noodles:
- Cook the rice noodles according to the package instructions. Drain and set aside.

Cook the Tofu:

- In a large skillet or wok, heat vegetable oil over medium-high heat. Add the cubed tofu and cook until all sides are golden brown. Remove from the skillet and set aside.

Sauté Vegetables:
- In the same skillet, add more oil if needed. Sauté bell pepper, julienned carrot, and snow peas until they are slightly tender but still crisp.

Combine and Toss:
- Add the cooked noodles and tofu to the skillet with sautéed vegetables.
- Pour the peanut sauce over the noodles and tofu. Toss everything together until well coated in the sauce.

Garnish:
- Garnish the Asian Peanut Noodles with Tofu with sliced green onions and sesame seeds.

Serve:
- Serve the noodles hot.

Enjoy:
- This dish is a flavorful and satisfying blend of noodles, tofu, and crisp vegetables with a delicious peanut sauce.

Freezing (Optional):
- Allow any leftovers to cool before transferring to freezer-safe containers.

This Asian Peanut Noodles with Tofu is a delicious and freezer-friendly option. Reheat it on the stovetop for a quick and tasty meal. Enjoy!

Baked Ziti

Ingredients:

- 1 lb ziti pasta
- 1 lb ground beef or Italian sausage
- 1 onion, finely chopped
- 3 cloves garlic, minced
- 1 can (28 oz) crushed tomatoes
- 1 can (15 oz) tomato sauce
- 1/2 cup red wine (optional)
- 2 teaspoons dried oregano
- 1 teaspoon dried basil
- Salt and black pepper to taste
- 2 cups ricotta cheese
- 1 egg
- 3 cups shredded mozzarella cheese
- 1 cup grated Parmesan cheese
- Fresh basil or parsley, chopped (for garnish)

Instructions:

Cook the Ziti:
- Cook the ziti pasta according to the package instructions. Drain and set aside.

Prepare the Meat Sauce:
- In a large skillet, cook the ground beef or Italian sausage over medium heat until browned. Add chopped onion and minced garlic and cook until the onion is softened.
- Stir in crushed tomatoes, tomato sauce, red wine (if using), dried oregano, dried basil, salt, and black pepper. Simmer the sauce for about 15-20 minutes, allowing the flavors to meld.

Preheat the Oven:
- Preheat your oven to 375°F (190°C).

Prepare the Ricotta Mixture:
- In a bowl, combine ricotta cheese and egg. Mix well until smooth.

Assemble the Baked Ziti:

- In a large mixing bowl, combine the cooked ziti with half of the meat sauce.
- In a baking dish, layer half of the ziti mixture. Dollop half of the ricotta mixture over the ziti, then sprinkle with half of the shredded mozzarella and Parmesan cheese.
- Repeat the layers with the remaining ziti, meat sauce, ricotta mixture, and cheeses.

Bake:
- Cover the baking dish with aluminum foil and bake in the preheated oven for 25 minutes.
- Remove the foil and bake for an additional 15 minutes or until the cheese is melted and bubbly, and the edges are golden.

Garnish and Serve:
- Remove from the oven and let it cool for a few minutes.
- Garnish with chopped fresh basil or parsley.
- Serve the Baked Ziti hot.

Enjoy:
- This classic baked ziti is a comforting and satisfying dish that's perfect for a family dinner.

Freezing (Optional):
- Allow any leftovers to cool before transferring to freezer-safe containers.

Baked Ziti is a great make-ahead dish that can be frozen for future meals. Reheat in the oven for a delicious and hearty dinner. Enjoy!

Moroccan Chickpea Stew

Ingredients:

- 2 tablespoons olive oil
- 1 onion, finely chopped
- 3 cloves garlic, minced
- 1 teaspoon ground cumin
- 1 teaspoon ground coriander
- 1 teaspoon ground cinnamon
- 1/2 teaspoon ground turmeric
- 1/2 teaspoon paprika
- 1/4 teaspoon cayenne pepper (adjust to taste)
- 1 can (15 oz) chickpeas, drained and rinsed
- 1 can (14 oz) diced tomatoes
- 1 cup vegetable broth
- 1 sweet potato, peeled and diced
- 2 carrots, peeled and sliced
- 1 zucchini, diced
- 1 red bell pepper, diced
- 1 cup frozen peas
- Salt and black pepper to taste
- Fresh cilantro, chopped (for garnish)
- Lemon wedges (for serving)
- Cooked couscous or rice (for serving)

Instructions:

Sauté Aromatics:
- In a large pot, heat olive oil over medium heat. Add chopped onion and cook until softened.
- Add minced garlic and sauté for an additional minute until fragrant.

Spice it Up:
- Stir in ground cumin, ground coriander, ground cinnamon, ground turmeric, paprika, and cayenne pepper. Cook for 1-2 minutes to toast the spices.

Add Chickpeas and Tomatoes:
- Add drained and rinsed chickpeas, diced tomatoes (with their juices), and vegetable broth to the pot. Bring to a simmer.

Incorporate Vegetables:

- Add diced sweet potato, sliced carrots, diced zucchini, and diced red bell pepper to the pot. Stir to combine.

Simmer:
- Cover the pot and let the stew simmer over medium-low heat for 20-25 minutes, or until the vegetables are tender.

Add Peas and Seasoning:
- Stir in frozen peas and cook for an additional 5 minutes.
- Season the stew with salt and black pepper to taste.

Garnish and Serve:
- Ladle the Moroccan Chickpea Stew over cooked couscous or rice.
- Garnish with chopped fresh cilantro.
- Serve hot with lemon wedges on the side for squeezing.

Enjoy:
- This flavorful and aromatic Moroccan Chickpea Stew is a hearty and nutritious meal.

Freezing (Optional):
- Allow any leftovers to cool before transferring to freezer-safe containers.

This Moroccan Chickpea Stew is a delicious and freezer-friendly option. Reheat it on the stovetop for a quick and flavorful meal. Enjoy!

Buffalo Chicken Wraps

Ingredients:

For the Buffalo Chicken:

- 1 lb boneless, skinless chicken breasts, cooked and shredded
- 1/2 cup buffalo sauce
- 2 tablespoons unsalted butter, melted
- 1 tablespoon honey (optional, for sweetness)
- Salt and black pepper to taste

For the Wraps:

- 4 large flour tortillas
- 1 cup shredded lettuce
- 1 cup diced tomatoes
- 1/2 cup diced red onion
- 1/2 cup crumbled blue cheese or ranch dressing
- Fresh cilantro or parsley, chopped (for garnish)

Instructions:

Prepare Buffalo Chicken:
- In a bowl, mix the shredded chicken with buffalo sauce, melted butter, honey (if using), salt, and black pepper. Toss until the chicken is well coated.

Assemble the Wraps:
- Lay out the flour tortillas on a flat surface.
- Divide the shredded lettuce, diced tomatoes, diced red onion, and buffalo chicken evenly among the tortillas.
- Sprinkle crumbled blue cheese or drizzle ranch dressing over the top.

Roll the Wraps:
- Fold in the sides of each tortilla and then roll them up tightly, creating a wrap.

Slice and Garnish:
- Slice each wrap in half diagonally.

- Garnish with chopped fresh cilantro or parsley.

Serve:
- Serve the Buffalo Chicken Wraps immediately.

Enjoy:
- These wraps are a perfect combination of spicy buffalo chicken, crisp vegetables, and creamy dressing.

Freezing (Optional):
- Allow any leftover buffalo chicken to cool before freezing. Assemble the wraps fresh when you're ready to eat.

Buffalo Chicken Wraps are a quick and flavorful meal that's perfect for lunch or dinner.

Enjoy the bold and zesty flavors in every bite!

Vegetarian Spinach and Mushroom Enchiladas

Ingredients:

For the Filling:

- 2 tablespoons olive oil
- 1 onion, finely chopped
- 2 cloves garlic, minced
- 8 oz mushrooms, sliced
- 4 cups fresh spinach, chopped
- 1 can (15 oz) black beans, drained and rinsed
- 1 teaspoon ground cumin
- 1 teaspoon chili powder
- Salt and black pepper to taste

For the Enchilada Sauce:

- 2 tablespoons olive oil
- 2 tablespoons all-purpose flour
- 3 tablespoons chili powder
- 1 teaspoon ground cumin
- 1/2 teaspoon garlic powder
- 1/4 teaspoon dried oregano
- 2 cups vegetable broth
- Salt to taste

For Assembly:

- 8 large flour tortillas
- 2 cups shredded Mexican blend cheese
- Fresh cilantro, chopped (for garnish)
- Sour cream (optional, for serving)
- Salsa (optional, for serving)
- Avocado slices (optional, for serving)

Instructions:

Prepare the Filling:

- In a large skillet, heat olive oil over medium heat. Add chopped onion and sauté until translucent.
- Add minced garlic and sliced mushrooms. Cook until the mushrooms release their moisture and become golden brown.
- Stir in chopped spinach and cook until wilted.
- Add drained black beans, ground cumin, chili powder, salt, and black pepper. Cook for an additional 2-3 minutes. Remove from heat.

Prepare the Enchilada Sauce:
- In a separate saucepan, heat olive oil over medium heat. Stir in all-purpose flour and cook for 1-2 minutes to create a roux.
- Add chili powder, ground cumin, garlic powder, dried oregano, and salt. Whisk in vegetable broth gradually, ensuring a smooth sauce. Simmer until the sauce thickens. Remove from heat.

Assemble the Enchiladas:
- Preheat the oven to 375°F (190°C).
- Spread a small amount of enchilada sauce in the bottom of a baking dish.
- Spoon the spinach and mushroom filling onto each tortilla, roll them up, and place them seam side down in the baking dish.
- Pour the remaining enchilada sauce over the top of the rolled tortillas.
- Sprinkle shredded cheese over the enchiladas.

Bake:
- Bake in the preheated oven for 20-25 minutes or until the cheese is melted and bubbly.

Garnish and Serve:
- Remove from the oven and garnish with chopped cilantro.
- Serve the Vegetarian Spinach and Mushroom Enchiladas hot.

Optional Toppings:
- Serve with sour cream, salsa, and avocado slices on the side.

Enjoy:
- These enchiladas are a delicious and satisfying vegetarian option.

Freezing (Optional):
- Allow any leftover enchiladas to cool before transferring to freezer-safe containers.

These Vegetarian Spinach and Mushroom Enchiladas are a flavorful and freezer-friendly dish. Reheat them in the oven for a convenient and delicious meal. Enjoy!

Cabbage Roll Casserole

Ingredients:

For the Filling:

- 1 lb ground beef or ground turkey
- 1 onion, finely chopped
- 2 cloves garlic, minced
- 1 cup rice, uncooked
- 1 can (14 oz) diced tomatoes
- 1 can (8 oz) tomato sauce
- 1 teaspoon dried oregano
- 1 teaspoon dried thyme
- Salt and black pepper to taste
- 1 head green cabbage, shredded

For the Sauce:

- 1 can (14 oz) crushed tomatoes
- 1 tablespoon brown sugar
- 1 tablespoon apple cider vinegar
- 1 teaspoon paprika
- Salt and black pepper to taste

For Assembly:

- 1 cup shredded mozzarella cheese
- Fresh parsley, chopped (for garnish)

Instructions:

Prepare the Filling:
- In a large skillet, brown the ground beef or turkey over medium heat. Drain excess fat if necessary.
- Add chopped onion and minced garlic. Sauté until the onion is softened.

- Stir in uncooked rice, diced tomatoes, tomato sauce, dried oregano, dried thyme, salt, and black pepper. Cook for 5-7 minutes or until the rice is partially cooked.
- Add shredded cabbage to the skillet. Cook until the cabbage is wilted and the filling is well combined.

Make the Sauce:
- In a separate bowl, mix crushed tomatoes, brown sugar, apple cider vinegar, paprika, salt, and black pepper.

Assemble the Casserole:
- Preheat the oven to 375°F (190°C).
- In a baking dish, spread a small amount of the tomato sauce on the bottom.
- Add half of the cabbage and meat mixture, then spread half of the remaining tomato sauce over it.
- Add the remaining cabbage and meat mixture and top with the rest of the tomato sauce.

Bake:
- Cover the baking dish with foil and bake in the preheated oven for 40-45 minutes or until the rice is fully cooked.

Cheese and Finish:
- Remove the foil and sprinkle shredded mozzarella cheese over the casserole.
- Bake for an additional 10-15 minutes or until the cheese is melted and bubbly.

Garnish and Serve:
- Remove from the oven and let it cool for a few minutes.
- Garnish with chopped fresh parsley.
- Serve the Cabbage Roll Casserole hot.

Enjoy:
- This casserole is a convenient way to enjoy the flavors of traditional cabbage rolls without the fuss.

Freezing (Optional):
- Allow any leftover casserole to cool before transferring to freezer-safe containers.

This Cabbage Roll Casserole is a hearty and freezer-friendly dish. Reheat it in the oven for a delicious and comforting meal. Enjoy!

Lemon Herb Grilled Chicken

Ingredients:

- 4 boneless, skinless chicken breasts
- Zest of 1 lemon
- Juice of 2 lemons
- 3 tablespoons olive oil
- 2 cloves garlic, minced
- 1 tablespoon fresh rosemary, chopped
- 1 tablespoon fresh thyme, chopped
- Salt and black pepper to taste
- Lemon slices (for garnish)
- Fresh parsley, chopped (for garnish)

Instructions:

Prepare the Marinade:
- In a bowl, combine lemon zest, lemon juice, olive oil, minced garlic, chopped rosemary, chopped thyme, salt, and black pepper.

Marinate the Chicken:
- Place the chicken breasts in a shallow dish or a large zip-top bag.
- Pour the marinade over the chicken, making sure each breast is well-coated.
- Marinate the chicken in the refrigerator for at least 30 minutes, or ideally, for a few hours to allow the flavors to infuse.

Preheat the Grill:
- Preheat your grill to medium-high heat.

Grill the Chicken:
- Remove the chicken from the marinade and shake off any excess.
- Grill the chicken breasts for about 6-8 minutes per side or until they reach an internal temperature of 165°F (74°C) and have a nice char on the outside.

Rest and Garnish:
- Remove the chicken from the grill and let it rest for a few minutes.
- Garnish with lemon slices and chopped fresh parsley.

Serve:
- Serve the Lemon Herb Grilled Chicken hot.

Enjoy:
- This grilled chicken is flavorful and aromatic, with a perfect balance of lemon and herbs.

Pairing Suggestion:
- Serve with a side of grilled vegetables, a refreshing salad, or your favorite grains.

Freezing (Optional):
- If you have leftover grilled chicken, allow it to cool before freezing. Reheat it in the oven or on the grill for a quick and tasty meal.

Enjoy your Lemon Herb Grilled Chicken!

Sweet and Sour Meatballs

Ingredients:

For the Meatballs:

- 1 lb ground beef or a combination of beef and pork
- 1/2 cup breadcrumbs
- 1/4 cup milk
- 1/4 cup finely chopped onion
- 1 clove garlic, minced
- 1 large egg
- Salt and black pepper to taste
- 2 tablespoons vegetable oil (for cooking)

For the Sweet and Sour Sauce:

- 1 cup pineapple juice
- 1/4 cup ketchup
- 3 tablespoons soy sauce
- 3 tablespoons brown sugar
- 2 tablespoons rice vinegar
- 1 tablespoon cornstarch
- 1/4 cup water

For Assembly:

- 1 bell pepper, cut into chunks
- 1 onion, cut into chunks
- 1 cup pineapple chunks (fresh or canned)
- Cooked rice (for serving)
- Green onions, sliced (for garnish, optional)
- Sesame seeds (for garnish, optional)

Instructions:

Prepare the Meatballs:

- In a large bowl, combine ground beef, breadcrumbs, milk, chopped onion, minced garlic, egg, salt, and black pepper. Mix until well combined.
- Shape the mixture into meatballs, approximately 1 inch in diameter.
- In a skillet, heat vegetable oil over medium heat. Cook the meatballs until browned on all sides and cooked through. Remove from the skillet and set aside.

Make the Sweet and Sour Sauce:
- In a bowl, whisk together pineapple juice, ketchup, soy sauce, brown sugar, and rice vinegar.
- In a small bowl, dissolve cornstarch in water to create a slurry.
- Pour the pineapple juice mixture into a saucepan. Heat over medium heat until it starts to simmer.
- Gradually whisk in the cornstarch slurry, stirring constantly until the sauce thickens. Remove from heat.

Combine Meatballs and Sauce:
- Place the cooked meatballs in the skillet or saucepan with the sweet and sour sauce.
- Add bell pepper chunks, onion chunks, and pineapple chunks to the mixture.
- Simmer over low heat for 10-15 minutes, allowing the flavors to meld and the vegetables to become tender.

Serve:
- Serve the Sweet and Sour Meatballs over cooked rice.

Garnish:
- Garnish with sliced green onions and sesame seeds if desired.

Enjoy:
- These Sweet and Sour Meatballs are a delightful balance of sweet, tangy, and savory flavors.

Optional Variation:
- You can also bake the meatballs in the oven instead of cooking them on the stovetop. Simply arrange them on a baking sheet and bake at 375°F (190°C) for 20-25 minutes or until cooked through.

Freezing (Optional):
- Allow any leftovers to cool before transferring to freezer-safe containers.

Enjoy your Sweet and Sour Meatballs!